Beautiful America's
Alaska

Text and Photography
by George Wuerthner

Contents

INTRODUCTION

Henry Gannett, director of the U.S. Geological Survey, wrote in a 1901 *National Geographic* article on Alaska that the state's scenery would eventually prove "more valuable than the gold or the fish or the timber, for it will never be exhausted." Gannett did not anticipate the role oil would play in today's society, but he was basically correct in his assertion, for tourism is currently Alaska's number two industry, and easily outdistances gold, fish, and timber in terms of economic importance.

Gannett was awestruck by Alaska's scenery and he advised potential Alaskan travelers: "If you are old, go by all means, but if you are young, stay away until you are older. The scenery of Alaska is so much grander than anything else of the kind in the world that, once beheld, all other scenery becomes flat and insipid. It is not well to dull one's capacity for such enjoyment by seeing the finest first."

Unfortunately for myself, I didn't heed Gannett's admonishment. I went to Alaska when I was nineteen. Gannett was correct. Alaska is in a class by itself. I've not found anyplace else in North America to surpass it for sheer dramatic effect, space, and wildness. Since my first trek north, I've been "forced" to return eighteen more times—Alaska's scenery and wildlife exuberance is addictive.

Of course, I was captivated by the lure of Alaska's wilderness at an early age. Even in grade school, I devoured books on this northern outpost of the nation. Many odd bits of Alaskan trivia I still carry with me today. The names of George Vancouver, Vitus Bering, James Cook, and William Dall were not only appellations on the map, but men as familiar to me as the baseball stars that claimed the interest of my peers. I read about the natives—the Indians and Eskimos who colonized the state long before the Europeans traveled north to "discover" it again. I studied Alaskan wildlife—learning that brown bears and grizzlies are the same animal. One lives along the coast, feeds on salmon, and grows large (brown bear). The other (grizzly) lives in the food-limited interior, getting by on roots and berries, or anything else it is lucky enough to catch. And though I could read about glaciers—rivers of ice the books called them—some like the Malaspina Glacier are larger than Rhode Island. It was almost beyond my imagination to conceive of a river of ice larger than a state. No wonder Alaska seemed bigger than life.

Sunset, downtown Anchorage

Alaska Statehood Park, Anchorage

Downtown Juneau

Governor's Mansion, Juneau

For me, and many others, that hasn't changed. Alaska grabs our hearts and minds. It is a land of vastness and extremes. Mountains so high, so long, so rugged they can swallow up entire sets of mountain ranges in the lower forty-eight states and still have room to spare. Rivers that roll for hundreds, if not thousands of miles, passing through virtual wilderness punctuated by a few isolated villages that claim no more than a few hundred inhabitants.

Within this huge region, there are dozens of mountain ranges, many with unnamed peaks and valleys, twelve major river systems and countless smaller creeks, three million lakes, and almost too many islands to count. A natural factor of extreme importance to the state is its coastline—some 34,000 miles of it—nearly 50 percent more seacoast than all of the continental United States combined!

The scale of the landscape is an inspiration to many, giving them opportunities to dream. This manifests itself in different ways. Early conservationist Bob Marshall proposed in the 1930s that everything north of the Yukon River be set aside as a huge wilderness park. And former governor Wally Hickel has advocated construction of a giant pipeline to send Alaska's abundant water to the Southwest U.S. to make the desert "bloom." Big thinkers, each in his own way.

I can't generalize about the entire state except to say it's huge. In land area it is larger than the twenty-one smaller states put together. Traveling from east to west spans 2,700 miles, nearly the distance from New York to San Francisco. And from its most southern point to its most northern is 1,400 miles—the same as traveling from Seattle to San Diego.

To people living in the coterminous forty-eight states, Alaska seems like it's hovering about the pole. Indeed, Anchorage lies another 1,445 air miles north of Seattle. Yet, much of Alaska is no farther north than northern Europe. Ketchikan lies near the same latitude as Hamburg. Olso and Anchorage are about an equal distance south of the pole. When we go west, we run into the same geographical peculiarities. From its westernmost point in the Bering Strait, you can see the coast of Russia. Honolulu is closer to the West Coast of the continental United States than Nome. Attu, the westernmost major island in the Aleutian chain, sits at the same longitude as New Zealand! Indeed, Alaska stretches so far west, it actually laps into the Eastern Hemisphere. If there were not a jog in the International Dateline to accommodate these islands, part of Alaska would be a day ahead of the rest of the state. From the extreme tip of this island chain, it is less than a thousand miles to Japan—a strategic fact that played an important role during World War II.

Because of its tremendous size and diversity of landscapes and climate, it's best to subdivide the state into a number of geographical regions. I'll discuss them in greater detail later in the book, but the following provides a brief overview. The "panhandle," or Southeast Alaska, takes in the island-studded archipelago adjacent to and north of British Columbia. The Coast Range forms a mountainous jumble of glacier-clad peaks along the eastern margin of the region, while much of the panhandle consists of thousands of forested islands. Major communities include Ketchikan, Sitka, and Juneau.

Anchorage forms the economic hub for Southcentral Alaska. Most of the region is an icy wilderness of giant mountain ranges like the Saint Elias, Chugach, and Kenai that rise dramatically from the sea. Despite the glaciers and mountains, Southcentral Alaska also supports the state's greatest human population centers. Besides Anchorage, other towns include Palmer, Wasilla, Kenai, Homer, Seward, Valdez, and Cordova. The famous Kenai Peninsula, playground to much of Alaska's urban population, lies within this subregion.

Southwest Alaska includes the volcanic Alaska Peninsula and Aleutian Islands. The climate is mild, cloudy, and stormy. Salmon easily outnumber people. Dutch Harbor and Naknek are among the larger communities.

The upper Yukon River drainage defines Alaska's Interior, cradled between the north slope of the Alaska Range and the south slope of the Brooks Range. Most of the landscape is forested and rolling, even flat, although the mountains that mark the boundaries of the Interior include Mount McKinley, highest in North America. Warm, sometimes hot, in the near twenty-four hours of sunshine in summer, and frigid in the winter, this region has the greatest climatic extremes of any in the state. The largest community is Fairbanks.

The Bering Sea, or Western Alaska, region includes Nome, Unalakleet, Bethel, and other communities that are largely populated by Eskimos. The delta regions of the Yukon and Kuskokwim Rivers are flat and watery, but the rest of the region is hilly, even mountainous. All of it borders the Bering Sea.

The Arctic region borders its namesake, the Arctic Ocean, and encompasses the entire northern portion of the state including the north slope of the Brooks Range.

Alaska Range near Broad Pass

Early morning in Ketchikan

Alaska spans such a great north-south distance that the amount of light experienced in winter and summer varies considerably. A common fallacy of "outsiders" is that all of Alaska is thrust into total darkness during the winter months. While it's true that the sun does not rise above the horizon for sixty-seven days in Point Barrow, Alaska's most northern locale, in more southern communities like Anchorage or Fairbanks the sun never entirely disappears. Even on the shortest day of the year in late December, Anchorage residents still receive some five-and-a-half hours of sunlight, while Fairbanks gets by on less than four hours of direct sun. However, this winter darkness is balanced by summer daylight. Anchorage basks in more than nineteen hours of summer light, while Barrow residents enjoy eighty-four days of continuous round-the-clock sunlight!

Just as the amount of light varies considerably across the breadth of the state, so does climate. Much of Alaska is surprisingly temperate. The state's southern reaches are washed in the warmth of the Japanese current, which produces an exceedingly mild climate given its northern location. Ketchikan's annual temperature is 46 degrees, about the same as communities along the Oregon coast. And Ketchikan's January average temperature of 35 degrees is 6 degrees warmer than Denver! Kodiak, further north but still bathed in warm ocean currents, has a January average of 33 degrees. Even Anchorage's January average temperature of 13 degrees is not that frosty, at least compared to cooler parts of the lower forty-eight states. For example, Westby, Montana averages 5 degrees in January.

Of course, there is reality to the Alaskan reputation for frigid temperatures. In the interior of Alaska, beyond the warming influence of the ocean, there is often crushing cold that numbs a person to the bone. The state's record low of minus 80 below zero was registered near the aptly named Coldfoot, on the southern slopes of the Brooks Range. The average January temperature in Fairbanks is a chilly minus 10, and a slightly cooler minus 14 at Point Barrow on the Arctic Ocean. And it is often much colder in these places. No one will argue with you if you suggest it's cold in the interior and Arctic reaches of Alaska.

While southern Alaskan communities experience relatively mild winter temperatures, they avoid exceptionally hot summer days as well. To use Ketchikan again, the July average is 58 degrees. So is the July average for Anchorage. This is identical to the July average experienced by Crested Butte, high in the Colorado Rockies. On the other hand, Fairbanks, lying in the protected interior and basking in nearly twenty-four hours of summer sunshine, can get quite warm. Temperatures in the high 90s are recorded almost every summer. Fort Yukon, north and east of Fairbanks on the Yukon River, holds the state record high of 100 degrees!

Precipitation varies even more than temperature. Barrow, on the Arctic Ocean, sits in a cold, frozen desert. Less than five inches of precipitation falls annually here. And even Fairbanks seldom exceeds ten inches of annual precipitation, which is less rainfall than the twelve inches that falls on Tucson, Arizona each year! The other end of the spectrum is represented by Ketchikan, in Alaska's rainy southeast region. More than 150 inches of precipitation is dumped on Ketchikan annually. Only a few coastal places in Oregon and Washington can match Alaska's Southeast region for the honor of rainiest place in the country.

Topography can greatly influence precipitation patterns. Anchorage lies in the "rain shadow" of the Chugach Mountains, receiving a scant fifteen inches of annual precipitation—the same as "sunny" Denver. Yet, less than twenty air miles away on the windward side of this coastal range lies the tiny community of Whittier, which is drenched by over 174 inches of precipitation a year. As wet as this might seem, Macleod Harbor in Prince William Sound, southeast of Anchorage, holds the state record for greatest annual precipitation, with 332 inches falling in 1976. That's almost an inch a day!

Given the alternatives, Anchorage has about the most appealing climate in Alaska. Not too frigid. Not too hot. Not too wet. This may account for the city's popularity. Indeed, more than 230,000 people call the "Big Village" home. Fairbanks, Alaska's second largest city, has 30,000 residents, 77,000 if surrounding communities and rural areas in the Fairbanks Borough are included. Juneau has some 25,000 people, while Ketchikan is fourth with around 8,000 residents. These four cities account for 75 percent of the state's population.

What is surprising to most people is that despite the myth of the sourdough, most Alaskans are urban dwellers. They live in regular frame houses, not cabins. They drive Subarus and Chevys, not dog sleds. Certainly, Anchorage has all the amenities of a large

(Opposite) Mount McKinley towers 20,320 feet, Denali National Park

Tanada Lake, Wrangell - St. Elias National Park

city, but even seemingly remote villages are increasingly part of the information highway. Most bush communities are linked to TV and telephone, as well as daily air service to and from major transportation hubs like Anchorage or Fairbanks.

The state's isolation has decreased in the face of modern transportation. You can fly from Seattle to Anchorage in five hours. And even Barrow, the northernmost community, is linked by jet with Fairbanks. Tourists fly to Barrow for lunch and are back in Fairbanks for dinner.

Of course, driving to Alaska is still a grind. The major access is the Alaska Highway, or "Alcan" (for Alaska-Canada) as it is sometimes called. The highway begins at Dawson Creek in British Columbia and travels 1,500 miles to Fairbanks. The highway was constructed as a military road to move supplies and equipment to what was Alaska Territory during World War II. Built in a record nine months, the highway was completed in 1942, and was the first road to link Alaska with the lower forty-eight states. More than fifty years later, it is still the major highway access. Although almost completely paved today, when I traveled the Alaska Highway north, the road was mostly dirt—rutted dirt. Blinding, choking clouds of dust in the sun. Slick mud in the rain. Potholes the whole way. It was perilous to travel faster than thirty-five miles per hour. Today, driving reasonably long days, one can travel its length in three days. Once in Alaska, your options are fairly limited. There are highways between Anchorage and Fairbanks, down to the Kenai Peninsula, and even north to the Arctic Ocean over the Dalton Highway, but almost everywhere else you have to fly.

Though many visitors think otherwise, you can't drive from Anchorage to Juneau or Ketchikan—unless you "drive" a boat. Southeast Alaska, isolated by fjords and the giant peaks of the Coast Range, is linked to the rest of the state by ferry and plane. State-operated ferries also carry passengers and vehicles to communities in Prince William Sound, Kodiak Island, and Southwest Alaska.

All this tends to reinforce the idea that Alaska was, and is, where the buck stops. The "last frontier," as the car license plates used to proclaim. Alaska is the last place you can drive in a car—or at least the most northern place in the United States. The Dalton Highway ends 300 miles north of the Arctic Circle at Prudhoe Bay on the Arctic Ocean.

(Opposite) Old Russian Cemetary, Baranof Island, Sitka National Historic Park

This IS the end of the road—where the pavement hits the ice. For many, Alaska is the last place they can make a buck, or live out a fantasy of being at the edge of humanity. For others, it's the last place where making a buck won't dictate all human actions, and the goal is to protect a "lasting" frontier in national parks, wildlife refuges, and wilderness areas. Such contrasts in attitudes, goals, and perspective exist everywhere, but there are few places where they are idiosyncratic of the people and land itself.

HISTORY

Historically, Alaska has always been something of a land of extremes. The native people arrived from Asia by way of the Bering Sea land bridge. First the paleo-Indians, followed in later migrations by Eskimos and Aleuts. The Indians were divided into a number of subgroups. Athabascan people settled the interior of Alaska along the major rivers like the upper Yukon and upper Kuskokwim. Tlingit Indians, makers of totem poles and war canoes, were found along the coasts of Southeast Alaska. Eskimos, traveling by kayak and umiak (a large, skin canoe) were largely coastal residents, settling along the seacoast all the way through Prince William Sound north to the Arctic. In some instances, they pushed inland into some of the major river valleys like the Kobuk and lower Yukon. Aleuts were found in their namesake area, the Aleutian Islands.

The densest settlement of native people was along the coasts; in part because food resources were greater here than in the interior. With salmon, sea mammals, shellfish, and other sources of food readily acquired, development of permanent villages was possible, and a greater degree of social structure existed. For example, in Southeast Alaska abundant food enabled people to spend time carving totem poles and constructing elaborate houses and canoes.

Alaska was put on the European map when the Dane Vitus Bering, sailing in a foggy haze, bumped into the coast of Alaska in 1741. Bering was working for the Russian Czar, Peter the Great, and claimed Alaska for Russia. Shortly after, Russian fur trappers began to plunder Alaskan waters, killing sea otters for their pelts and enslaving the native people at the same time. By 1784, a permanent Russian settlement was established on Kodiak Island. Later the Russians established other forts and settlements, including those on the Kenai Peninsula and at Sitka in Southeast Alaska. Colonialism and religion were always intertwined, and with the Russians came the Russian Orthodox Church, with forty of the onion-domed churches eventually being built in the state.

Explorers from other nations also coasted along Alaska's shores. Sea captains like the Englishmen Cook and Vancouver, Italians like Malaspina, Spaniards like Perez, along with the Russians, left a rich legacy of names upon Alaska's landscape. Cook Inlet, Admiralty Island, Lynn Canal, Prince William Sound, Valdez, Chichagof Island, Kachemak Bay, and Malaspina Glacier reflect these different national interests.

The Russians held Alaska for 126 years. It was, in essence, the "Siberia" of its time, a remote backwater of the Russian empire. The parent country didn't expend much money or energy improving or exploring its colony. Although the major features of the Alaskan coast were charted by the early 1800s, the interior of Alaska was largely unexplored. It wasn't until the 1820-1840s that Russians penetrated the lower reaches of the Yukon, Kuskokwim, and other rivers. However, much of the vast interior remained unknown and uncharted territory until late into the 1800s, even into the 1900s.

By the 1840s, trapping had so depleted furbearer stocks that Alaska had become a nearly forgotten frontier outpost. Seeing no further reason to hold on to its far-flung colony, Russia had a chance to dump what it perceived to be its worthless Alaskan holdings in 1867. Entering into negotiations with Secretary of State William Henry Seward, Russia sold the entire territory to the United States for little more than five cents an acre, or a total cost of $7.2 million. Many in the U.S. Congress were unimpressed with Seward's proposed purchase, calling it "Icebergia," "Walrussia," and "Seward's Folly." The treaty to purchase the territory only passed the Senate by three votes.

Indeed, initially the Russians thought they got the better end of the deal. But just a short five years later, in 1872, gold was discovered in Southeast Alaska. In rapid succession, other discoveries were made at Windham, Juneau, and elsewhere. Seward's Folly was now beginning to look like "Seward's Gold Mine." The stampede north was on. It culminated in 1897 when gold was discovered in the Klondike (which was in the Yukon

Chilkoot Lake State Recreation Area near Haines

Klehini River, Chilkat Bald Eagle Preserve

Territory), and more than a hundred thousand people converged on the gold fields. Most got there too late to stake a viable claim. The vast majority soon left, headed back to wherever they came from, but a few stayed on, and spread out across the vast landscape looking for other gold fields. They found a few. Gold was discovered in Nome (1899), Fairbanks (1902), Innoko (1906), Ruby (1907), Iditarod (1908), Wiseman (1910), and Livengood (1914). The peak for gold production was 1906. Most of these gold rush towns disappeared after a few years of mineral exploitation, but a few lingered to become respectable cities, including Fairbanks and Nome.

The gold rush revived American interest in the state. Congress finally began to pay attention to its far northern outpost and granted territorial status in 1912. The heady days of the gold rush began to fade, and Alaska slid into a long economic decline. One of the few bright spots was the construction of the Alaskan Railroad, authorized by President Wilson in 1914. The railroad wasn't completed until 1923. The tracks ran from Seward north to Fairbanks. Anchorage got its start in 1915 as a tent camp, housing construction workers who were helping to build the railroad.

Alaska's waters were rich in fish, particularly salmon. The first canneries were established in Southeast Alaska in 1878. Gradually the fishing industry grew. The salmon industry peaked in the 1930s, then nearly collapsed. Since then, the fishing industry has diversified and has come under increasingly stricter regulation. Besides salmon, fishermen now capture shellfish and bottomfish, but it's questionable whether current fishing levels can be sustained in the long run.

Alaska's economy was rescued after the fishing industry's collapse by World War II. Alaska's strategic position in the Pacific theater was recognized early. Even before war broke out with Japan, the United States began fortifying the state as a military staging ground. New airfields were constructed and harbors fortified. By late 1942, more than 150,000 troops were stationed in Alaska, and the Alaska Highway was constructed, in a record nine months, to provide for the rapid movement of troops and supplies to Alaska by a non-water route.

Additional fortification was prompted by the June 2, 1942 Japanese invasion. Japanese planes bombed Dutch Harbor. Soldiers stormed Attu and Kiska, further west in the

Aleutians, and occupied the islands for almost a year. On May 11, 1943, American troops advanced on Attu. By May 29th, the Japanese made a banzai attack, losing nearly all of their men—most Japanese soldiers committed suicide rather than surrender. All together 2,351 Japanese dead were counted. Victory, such as it was, cost the Americans as well. There were 3,829 casualties, the second greatest number of American losses in the Pacific after Iwo Jima.

The Japanese were driven out of Alaska by 1943. The military buildup and presence in Alaska, however, continued throughout the 1950s, 1960s and 1970s to counter the threat that the Soviet Union was thought to pose to U.S. security. For decades, the military was a pillar of Alaska's economy, providing a relatively stable economic base. It remains so today.

Just after the turn of the century, the coastal forests of Southeast and Southcentral Alaska were given some protection as part of the newly established Tongass and Chugach National Forests. Today the Tongass encompasses 17 million acres, or nearly the size of the state of Maine. The Chugach National Forest is considerably smaller, taking in only 5.9 million acres, but this is still nearly the size of the state of Vermont! During the 1950s Alaska's timber industry really took off. With generous terms and long-term contracts with the U.S. Forest Service, several large pulp mills were constructed in Southeast Alaska to take advantage of the region's abundant and (thanks to taxpayer subsidies) cheap timber. As huge clearcuts spread across the forested islands of Southeast Alaska, logging came under increasing scrutiny from environmentalists as well as groups like the National Taxpayers Union. Responding to growing protest, in 1990 Congress passed the Tongass Reform Act, eliminating a $40 million annual subsidy that promoted logging, and the mandated minimum annual cut of 450 million board feet. Some of the Tongass's spectacular scenery has been put beyond the reach of the logger's saw as designated wilderness, including Tracy Arms-Fords Terror Wilderness, West Chichagof Wilderness, Admiralty Island National Monument, and Misty Fiords National Monument.

With its strategic location assured, and its population stabilized, Alaska was admitted to the union as the forty-ninth state in 1959. Perhaps feeling a bit of guilt for nearly one hundred years of benign neglect, Congress was extremely generous to Alaska at statehood. The state was granted control of many federally-built developments, including

Boat harbor, Seward

Start of Iditarod Trail, Seward

Sled dog demonstration

Alaskan sled dog

25

harbors, airfields, and old military bases, plus given title to more than 104 million acres of federally controlled land—an area approximately equal in size to the state of California. This surpassed the amount of land conferred upon all seventeen western states combined. In addition, Alaska was given rights to 90 percent of the royalties from federal mineral leases compared to the 25 percent enjoyed by most states. This last provision, in particular, proved a boom to the state once oil was discovered in huge quantities on the North Slope.

Indeed, it was oil, more than any other factor, that made modern Alaska. That Alaska harbored substantial reserves of oil had been known for decades. However, the distance to markets and the great cost of development, not a lack of oil, slowed oil exploitation in the state. The first Alaskan oil well was drilled in 1898, the same year as the Klondike gold rush. The first commercial well was drilled in 1902 at Katalla, east of Cordova, but again, a lack of markets precluded extensive development. In 1923, the federal government set aside the Naval Petroleum Reserve (now known as the National Petroleum Reserve) along Alaska's North Slope south of Point Barrow. Significant commercial development began when the Swanson River oilfield was established in 1957 on the Kenai Peninsula and Cooke Inlet south of Anchorage. But it was the big discovery at Prudhoe Bay, along the Arctic Ocean on Alaska's North Slope in 1968, that catapulted Alaska into the role of a major oil producer. The Prudhoe Bay field was not an ordinary find. It was the largest field in North America, and the tenth biggest oil discovery in the world. All other large fields are in the Middle East. The extraordinary size of the Prudhoe Bay oil deposits, containing one quarter of the total oil reserves in the United States, justified the huge expense of development in a remote and hostile working environment. By 1987, Alaska surpassed Texas as the number one oil producer in the nation.

Having oil in the ground doesn't mean much if you can't get it to markets. That's where the Trans Alaska Pipeline played a pivotal role in Alaska's oil development. The pipeline was built for a cost of $8 billion. Completed in 1976, after three frantic years of work, the 800-mile-long pipeline begins at Prudhoe Bay on the North Slope and terminates at Valdez, a small, ice-free port in Prince William Sound. Here, tankers take the oil to refineries in the lower forty-eight states.

Permission to construct the pipeline was initially stalled by long-standing land claims of Alaska's native people. Before the oil companies could be given clearance to build their pipeline the native claims had to be resolved. The issue of pipeline construction made unlikely allies of the natives and the oil companies, who jointly went to Congress to ask for a hasty resolution. In 1971, the Alaska Native Claims Settlement Act (or ANCSA) passed Congress. In exchange for final extinguishment of any future claims, Congress granted Alaska's native people claim to 44 million acres of land (approximately the size of all New England), plus one billion dollars in cash. Nine native corporations were set up to manage land and other assets. Villages, as well as each native person, were given title to land. Alaska's native corporations invested in everything from hotels in Anchorage to logging operations in Southeast Alaska to oil production on Alaska's North Slope. Some native corporations have prospered. For example, Arctic Slope Native Corporation controls mineral rights to much of the land beneath the North Slope oil fields, and has enjoyed tremendous profits as a consequence of oil development. Indeed, in some cases the interests of Alaska's native people and the oil companies still seem bound together. For example, the Arctic Slope Native Corporation and other native corporations have invested in oil development. They, along with the oil companies, are currently lobbying Congress to open up the Arctic Wildlife Refuge to oil development.

With the land claims extinguished, the path was cleared for an oil pipeline right-of-way. Construction of the great Alaskan pipeline began almost immediately.

Portions of the pipeline were built aboveground to allow for animal migrations, as well as to prevent thawing of permafrost which underlay much of the pipeline route. For the most part, the pipeline has operated with a minimum of problems. However, the 1989 wreak of the tanker *Exxon Valdez* in Prince William Sound, spilling oil across much of the southern Alaska coast, demonstrated that the transportation of oil is not without serious environmental risk.

Pipeline construction bought an era of prosperity to Alaska. Thousands moved north to take high-paying jobs doing everything from welding the huge pieces of pipe together to cooking in the numerous construction camps located along the route. Fairbanks in particular boomed, with skyrocketing housing prices, overcrowded facilities, and rising crime.

Alaska's government and most of her citizens have generally supported greater oil

Sunrise on Port Wells, Chugach Mountains

(Opposite) Icebergs in Bearlake, Kenai Fjords

development and exploitation, in part because the state realizes tremendous profits from royalty payments—as mentioned earlier, a much higher percentage than that allotted to other states. Indeed, in the late 1980s some oil royalties accounted for 85 percent of Alaska's state government revenues. With a downturn in oil prices in the late 1980s, Alaska's state government faced serious financial difficulties as royalty revenues dropped.

ANCSA has other long-term consequences for Alaska's future. One small subsection of the act called upon the U.S. Secretary of the Interior to select lands from the public domain to be designated national parks. During the height of the pipeline boom years, studies were undertaken to determine which lands should be set aside for conservation purposes. Alaska's congressional delegation and state officials were vigorously opposed to any new conservation units, arguing that they would destroy the state's economy. Such claims are not new. In 1924, when Glacier Bay was first set aside as a national monument, the *Juneau Empire* suggested in an editorial that protecting the bay was "the quintessence of silliness. It leads one to wonder if Washington has gone crazy through catering to conservation faddists." Of course, today Glacier Bay is one of the prime attractions for Southeast Alaska's tourist industry.

Despite the failure of past predictions of economic chaos due to conservation land protection to materialize, new park designations proposed in the 1970s were opposed by many Alaskans. The state's congressional delegation did everything it could to derail proposed conservation legislation. Fortunately for Alaska, as well as the rest of the nation, parochial shortsightedness was overwhelmed by tremendous national support. Indeed, one of the last things President Jimmy Carter did while in office was sign, in December of 1980, the Alaska National Interest Lands Conservation Act (ANILCA), setting aside 106 million acres of new national parks, preserves, monuments, and wildlife refuges. In addition, some preexisting units like Denali National Park and Glacier National Park were expanded. Altogether 130 million acres were affected by the bill. It was the most sweeping conservation legislation ever passed by Congress.

The new legislation nearly doubled the size of Mt. McKinley National Park and changed its name to Denali. Both Katmai National Monument and Glacier Bay National Monument were enlarged and upgraded to national park status. Other new parks established by the 1980 legislation included Wrangell-St. Elias National Park and Preserve, Yukon-Charley Rivers National Preserve, Gates of the Arctic National Park and Preserve, Kobuk Valley National Park, Noatak National Preserve, Cape Krusenstern National Monument, Bering Land Bridge National Preserve, Aniakchak National Monument and Preserve, Admiralty Island National Monument, Misty Fiords National Monument, plus many new and significant wildlife refuges like Yukon Delta National Wildlife Refuge, an expanded Arctic National Wildlife Refuge, and others.

In Alaska today, the Bureau of Land Management manages 92 million acres, the National Park Service 50 million acres, the U.S. Fish and Wildlife Service (which manages wildlife refuges) 75.4 million acres, and the U.S. Forest Service 23.2 million acres. The state of Alaska controls another 85 million acres, while native people own 35 million acres, making them the largest private landowners in the state.

The designation of Alaska's new parks helped to fuel tourism in the state. Despite dire predictions that parks would "lock up" Alaska and destroy the state's economy, by the 1990s tourism was the second leading industry in the state. Of all the state's sources of income and employment, tourism appears to be the one that may provide long-term economic stability, as Gannett predicted at the turn of the century.

In the past, Alaska's economy has always been boom or bust, or maintained by federal government largesse. Fur was the first resource to lure outsiders to the state. It led to Russia's control of the fur trade, which was soon overexploited. Just when the few settlements based upon the fur trade seemed likely to disappear, the first gold was discovered. The gold rush was followed by salmon fishing, with the state's greatest catch occurring in the 1930s. After the fish stocks declined, Alaska was rescued from depopulation and financial ruin when its strategic value was realized during World War II. The military buildup fueled Alaska's economy into the 1970s, when it was overshadowed by oil. The pipeline years had faded by the 1990s into the tourist rush, as Alaska capitalizes upon its position as one of the world's major repositories for national parks.

Mount Muir, Harriman Fjord, Prince William Sound

32

THE REGIONS:
Southeast Alaska

I once saw a joke on the wall in a cabin by Glacier Bay National Park in Southeast Alaska. It said: "You can tell when it's summer in Southeast Alaska—the rain is warmer." And indeed, if anything is characteristic of this part of Alaska, it's the moisture that comes from the sky more or less continuously. If it isn't raining, it's getting ready to rain—so say the natives. If the sun shines, some businesses give employees the day off. Of course, like all generalities, there are exceptions. Once while kayaking Glacier Bay, I endured thirteen straight days of sunshine. And I mean endured. No one brings suntan lotion to Southeast Alaska and I was no exception. The intensity of sunshine was heightened by reflection off the water, and the nearly twenty hours of summer sunshine. There seemed to be no getting away from the sun. By the end of that sunny streak, I was so burnt I had to keep my face covered with a bandanna all day long.

The abundant rain sustains lush rainforests of Sitka spruce and western hemlock, with forests covering three quarters of the region—much of it part of the 17-million-acre Tongass National Forest. The forests and waterways support the densest population of bald eagles on earth, along with abundant salmon, whales, brown bear, and a host of other wildlife.

Bounded by the Coast Mountains along the border with British Columbia and the Fairweather Range on the north by Glacier Bay, some of Southeast Alaska's mountains rise nearly three miles in vertical relief! The rest of the 500-mile-long region consists of thousands of islands, including Prince of Wales Island, the third largest island in the nation. The entire region was overrun by glaciers during the last ice age, and the rivers of ice have carved deep fjords. Even today, the heavy winter snows—up to 400 inches may fall in some locations—feed huge icefields such as the Juneau Icefield that spawns the well-known Mendenhall Glacier by Juneau.

No place in Southeast Alaska is very far from the sea. The ocean helps to moderate the climate—average temperature in summer is in the sixties, while winters average in the twenties and thirties. Although mild overall, there are differences from place to place.

Moose in Horseshoe Pond, Denali National Park

Dall Sheep Rams, Denali National Park

Caribou Bull, Denali National Park

A south-north gradient prevails with the greatest rainfall in the south, and corresponding-ly less further north. For example, while Port Baker on the south end of Prince of Wales Island gets more than two hundred inches of precipitation annually, Skagway at the northern end of the mountain-rimmed Lynn Canal gets less than thirty inches—approximately half what Miami, Florida receives in a typical year.

The sea and forest have always provided for the area's residents. The Tlingit Indians depended upon the abundant salmon and other fish that swim in the region's waters for the mainstay of their diet. Fish, along with berries, sea mammals, and other foods provided native residents with plenty of resources, ensuring a relatively easy lifestyle.

Ketchikan is the first community encountered by people coming to Alaska by ferry. Located on the southwest side of Revillagigedo Island, Ketchikan is ninety miles north of Prince Rupert, British Columbia. It is one of the rainiest communities in Southeast Alaska, receiving over 160 inches of precipitation annually. October is the wettest month, while June is the driest. Local attractions include the totem pole parks—Totem Bight State Park and Saxman State Park. Ketchikan's economic well-being was strongly linked to logging, but like most of Southeast Alaska, its share of tourism is increasing, particularly since it is the gateway to the dramatic 2.3-million-acre Misty Fiords National Monument. Granite-walled fjords and heavily timbered valleys provide outstanding scenery comparable to Norway's famed coastline. Numerous boat charters are available in Ketchikan that cruise the narrow waterways of the monument.

Sitka, one of Southeast's major communities, was built on the site of a Tlingit Indian village. Sitka got its start when Alexander Baranof, of the Russian American Fur company, moved his company's headquarters from Kodiak to Sitka. Today, the Sitka Historical Park preserves both the Tlingit and Russian heritage. You can view totem poles that line the trail to a Russian fort site. On the site, you can see St. Michael's Cathedral, a Russian bishop's house, and an old Russian blockhouse. Sitka is also home to Sheldon Jackson College, a small private liberal arts school that specializes in marine biology and environmental studies.

Sitka was the base for the first few prospectors who explored Southeast Alaska for mineral riches in the early days. From the old Russian settlement, miners fanned out over the rest of the region looking for gold. Following discoveries at Windham Bay and elsewhere, two Sitka-based prospectors, Joe Juneau and Richard Harris, hit it rich near the mouth of Gold Creek on Gastineau Channel. Soon a town, now known as Juneau, sprang up on the site. Dubbed a "little San Francisco," Juneau clings to the steep side of 3,800-foot Mount Juneau. Downtown walking tours of its historic district, governor's mansion, and the Alaska State Museum are among the major attractions for the numerous tour boats that dock here annually.

With mountains out its back door, hiking trails radiate from downtown, including the 3.7-mile trail up Mount Roberts, which on a clear day affords commanding views of the Lynn Canal and peaks by Glacier Bay. Some thirteen miles from downtown Juneau is another local attraction, the Mendenhall Glacier. The glacier is fed by the abundant precipitation which varies considerably due to local topography. In town, annual precipitation is over ninety inches a year, while a few miles away at the airport, only fifty-four inches of precipitation falls annually.

Although mining was the reason Juneau was established, tourism and state government are its economic mainstays today. The state government was transferred to Juneau in 1906. Although there have been several attempts to move the capital to Southcentral Alaska, none have yet succeeded.

Juneau is also the usual jumping-off point for travelers to Admiralty Island National Monument. Admiralty Island is home to 3,000 nesting pairs of bald eagles and has the densest brown bear population in the world. The thick forests were once jeopardized by the largest proposed U.S. Forest Service timber sale in history; however, local conservationists succeeded in getting most of the island set aside as a national monument. Unfortunately, native-owned holdings on the island have been logged off in recent years, somewhat negating the attempts at preservation.

Haines is located at the north end of the long, glacially carved fjord now known as Lynn Canal. Haines guards the entrance to the Chilkat Valley, which was one of the important trade routes into the interior of the Yukon. The Chilkat Indians controlled this trade route, acting as middlemen in aboriginal trading ventures. A mission was established here in 1881, and later Fort William Seward was constructed. Today the fort is

Rafters on Fortymile Wild and Scenic River

Autumn color along Fortymile Wild and Scenic River

Sunset on Tanana River near Tanacross

a major tourist attraction in the town.

Haines also has much in the way of wildlife watching. In particular, a late fall run of chum salmon supports a thriving bald eagle population that gathers by the thousands to feast on the fish. The 48,000-acre Alaska Chilkat Bald Eagle Preserve was established in 1982 to preserve the roosting habitat of these magnificent birds.

Just 18 miles further up the fjord from Haines is the community of Skagway. Skagway is a town that thrives today because of its past. The town grew up on a narrow piece of flat ground where gold seekers unloaded their boats in preparation for crossing the Coast Mountains on their way to the Klondike. Today, the old false front stores of the downtown district have been restored as part of Klondike Gold Rush National Historic Park. Skagway is also the jumping-off point for the 33-mile Chilkoot Trail, once hiked by thousands of gold seekers in the winter of 1898.

The most popular scenic attraction in highly scenic Southeast Alaska is 3.3-million-acre Glacier Bay National Park. When Captain George Vancouver explored Icy Strait in 1794, what is now Glacier Bay was a 4,000-foot-high wall of ice. There was no bay. Since then, the glacier that once blocked the bay entrance has receded more than seventy-five miles. By the time naturalist John Muir visited Glacier Bay in 1879 and 1880, the ice had retreated some forty-five miles. Muir's writings brought national attention to the bay. The area was first protected as a national monument in the 1920s, and upgraded and enlarged to national park status in 1980. Today, visitors can see sixteen active tidewater glaciers that calve icebergs into the seventy-five mile long bay.

Southcentral Alaska

Southcentral Alaska takes in a curving 600 miles of Alaska, bordered on the south by the Gulf of Alaska and on the north by the Alaska Range. It includes Prince William Sound and the famous Kenai Peninsula. Some two-thirds of the state's population lives in this region, including Anchorage, Alaska's largest city. Other larger communities include Kodiak, Soldotna, Kenai, Homer, Seward, Palmer, and Wasilla.

A seismically active zone, Southcentral Alaska receives the bulk of Alaska's earthquake activity. The best known is the 1964 Alaskan earthquake, now thought to measure more than 9.2 on the Richter Scale—and the strongest earthquake ever recorded in the United States—releasing eighty times the energy of the 1906 San Francisco earthquake. The earthquake devastated Anchorage, as well as other communities like Kodiak. The quake and resulting seismic wave killed 118 people, with the greatest number of deaths in the tiny Prince William Sound community of Chenega, where 23 people died.

The earthquakes indicate that the region's mountains are still growing, and this region includes the higher peaks of the Alaska Range, which embraces 20,320-foot Mt. McKinley, the Talkeetna Mountains, the 16,000-foot-plus peaks of the Wrangell Mountains, the slightly lower Chugach Mountains, whose highest peak, Mount Marcus Baker, soars to 13,176 feet, and the Kenai Mountains, which rise to 6,600 feet. Kodiak Island rounds out the region. Major rivers include the Copper, Susitna, and Matanuska.

Southcentral Alaska is a transition zone. The coastal fringe is as wet as anyplace in southeast Alaska, yet just beyond the peaks of the Chugach Mountains lie the drier interior forests with aspen, birch, white spruce, and black spruce.

Of all Alaska's communities, Anchorage is the best known, and for good reason. Set at the head of Cook Inlet on flats at the base of the Chugach Mountains, with incredible views of the Alaska Range and Mt. McKinley, Anchorage has one of the most magnificent natural settings of any city its size in the United States. Alaska's largest city, Anchorage is home to more than half of the state's population, and is the center for commerce and transportation in the state. The economy is diverse and buoyed by federal and state offices, oil, the military, and tourism. First time visitors are often surprised by the city's modern appearance and facilities, with tall buildings flanked by parks, bike paths, and ski trails.

Many Alaskan residents like to say that Anchorage is not far from the real Alaska—whatever that may be. But one thing is certain, wildlife and magnificent country is not far from the town. Moose, salmon, wolves, and grizzlies can all be seen within twenty miles or less from downtown. Indeed, spawning salmon can be seen in Ship Creek, which flows through downtown Anchorage.

Many Anchorage residents use planes to get to the "real" Alaska. With half of the

Cabin near old mining town of Denali, Susitna River Valley

Tundra Lake and McLaren Glacier, Alaska Range

43

state's licensed pilots, it's not surprising that the city's two small airplane bases are the busiest in the nation. One of these small plane airports, Merrill Field, accounts for 25 percent of the state's take-offs and landings.

When Anchorage residents clear out for the weekend, they head for the Kenai Peninsula. So many cars hit the highway heading south, that a friend of mine jokingly dubbed it the Kenai 200. "People drive 200 miles south to Homer for the weekend, set out their lawn chairs, fish and crab, then drive 200 miles back to Anchorage."

The Kenai was the site of some of Alaska's earliest Russian settlements and reminders of this period can be seen in some of the names and Russian churches scattered about the region. Seward, on Resurrection Bay, is the terminus of the Alaskan Railroad, while Soldotna and Kenai were towns that grew due to oil development on the peninsula.

If Alaska has a rustic version of Santa Fe, then the village of Homer on Kachemak Bay might get the title. Well-known as a fishing village, its reputation as an artist's community is increasingly growing, and the town features several art galleries. Homer has what many consider to be a delightful climate. Protected from temperature extremes by sheltering mountains, warmed by the ocean, Homer seldom experiences temperatures above eighty degrees in summer, and almost never below zero in winter.

However, the main attraction of the Kenai is recreation. With numerous lakes, and famous salmon fishing in such rivers as the Kenai, Anchor River, and others, the Kenai is a fisherman's paradise. In addition to fishing, there is hiking on numerous trails in the Chugach National Forest as well as Kenai National Wildlife Refuge.

For those of a less ambitious inclination, the drive along the 127-mile-long Seward Highway, a designated national scenic byway, offers spectacular views of glacial fjords, lakes, and peaks. Portage Glacier, at the head of Turnagin Arm, is one of the state's biggest tourist attractions. However, Portage Glacier is not the only place to see these icy rivers. At the terminus of the Seward Highway in Seward, Alaska, one can board a boat for a ride into Kenai Fjords National Park. The 580,000-acre park encompasses numerous tidewater glaciers, as well as 300-square-mile Harding Icefield supported by snowfalls that may exceed 1,000 inches a year. Wildlife in the park includes humpback whales, sea otters, mountain goats, black bear, and bald eagles.

Seward and Homer both offer ferry service to Kodiak on 100-mile-long Kodiak Island—Alaska's largest island. The mountains of Kodiak are a southern extension of the Chugach Range. Kodiak, established by Russians, is the oldest permanent white settlement in Alaska. Commercial fishing is sustained by the rich waters surrounding the island, and catches of crab, salmon, and halibut helped Kodiak achieve its rank as the number one commercial fishing port in the state.

Most of the emerald-green island is part of the 1.9-million-acre Kodiak National Wildlife Refuge, set aside to protect the island's most famous residents—its large Alaskan brown bears. No place on the island is more than fifteen miles from the sea, and the abundant rainfall supports numerous short rivers that are jammed with salmon during spawning season.

East of Portage and the Kenai Peninsula's well-traveled highways lies glacier-studded Prince William Sound. Kayaking and boating are particularly attractive here. Similar to Southeast Alaska both in climate and topography, with numerous islands, Prince William Sound differs in having a lower treeline, with less extensive forests. Prince William Sound hosts twenty tidewater glaciers, including the large Columbia Glacier, which is accessible by tour boat from Valdez. Named for Columbia University by the 1899 Harriman Expedition, Columbia Glacier is forty miles long, and has a six-mile-wide snout. In recent years, the glacier has retreated more than a mile.

Taking in some of the most inaccessible portion of the coast, including Alaska's largest glaciers, is the immense 13.2-million-acre Wrangell-St. Elias National Park and Preserve. Malaspina Glacier is larger than the state of Rhode Island. The park has the greatest concentration of peaks exceeding 14,000 feet in North America and contains nine of the sixteen highest peaks in the United States. Many of the highest peaks—including Mt. Wrangell, Mt. Sanford, and Mt. Drum—are volcanoes.

Arctic Ground Squirrel, Denali National Park

Gray Wolf, Canis lupus

Sea lions, Aialik Bay, Kenai Peninsula

Southwestern Alaska

To anyone visiting Southwestern Alaska today, particularly the more remote Aleutian Islands, it may be difficult to understand why anyone would fight over these green, but misty, islands. Sandwiched between two of the stormiest seas on earth, the Bering Sea and the Gulf of Alaska, the area is notorious for its windy, rainy, damp climate. The weather is, by any standard, lousy. Some islands receive fewer than thirty sunny days a year.

Yet strategically, there can be no denying that controlling the Aleutians means controlling the North Pacific and the back door into the United States. It was exactly this strategic advantage that the Japanese hoped to capitalize upon when they invaded the Aleutians during World War II. Overall, the battle over the Aleutians was the second most costly fight in the Pacific theater, costing Americans nearly 4,000 casualties.

Today, the battle over the Aleutians seems almost forgotten. Now one of the most remote and least-populated parts of Alaska, the entire stormbound region is best known for its exceptional geological, archaeological, and wildlife values. Not surprisingly, there are significant holdings as wildlife refuges, preserves, and parks.

The 500-mile Alaska Peninsula, along with the Aleutian Islands that extend more than 1,000 miles out into the Pacific, makes up what is sometimes referred to as Southwest Alaska. Named for the Aleut people who call this region home, the Aleutians and adjacent Alaska Peninsula provide an abundance of resources for native people including fish, crab, whales, as well as land mammals.

The landscape is dominated by a string of active volcanoes set off by the Aleutian Trench, which marks where the Pacific plate is being subducted under the North American plate. The melting of plate margins feeds the 1,400-mile-long string of volcanoes that line the peninsula and Aleutian chain. Pavlof Volcano has erupted forty-one times since 1760! More recent eruptions of Augustine Volcano in Cook Inlet spewed ash over many of southern Alaska's settlements. And the eruption in 1989 of Mount Redoubt across Cook Inlet reminded many Alaskan residents of the unstable nature of this landscape.

One of the most famous volcanic displays occurred in June of 1912 in what is now Katmai National Park and Preserve when Novarupta Volcano, adjacent to Mount Katmai,

Stranded iceberg in Muir Inlet, Glacier Bay National Park

Saxman Totem Park, Ketchikan

Sternwheeler "Discovery" on Chena River, Fairbanks

Glacier Bay National Park

Wrangell Mountains near Nabesna

Sunrise over Muir Inlet

Fort Chilkoot, Haines

(Opposite) Copper River and Mount Sanford

Humpback Whales, Icy Strait

Skagway, Klondike Gold Rush National Historic Park

House at old Fort Seward, Haines

Bald Eagle, Glacier Bay National Park

Mount Drum, Wrangell Mountains

Seal pup, Muir Inlet, Glacier Bay National Park

61

Aleutian Range, Katmai National Park

Float plane on Naknek Lake, Katmai National Park

Grizzly bear on lake shore

(Opposite) Salmon jumping Brooks Falls, Katmai National Park

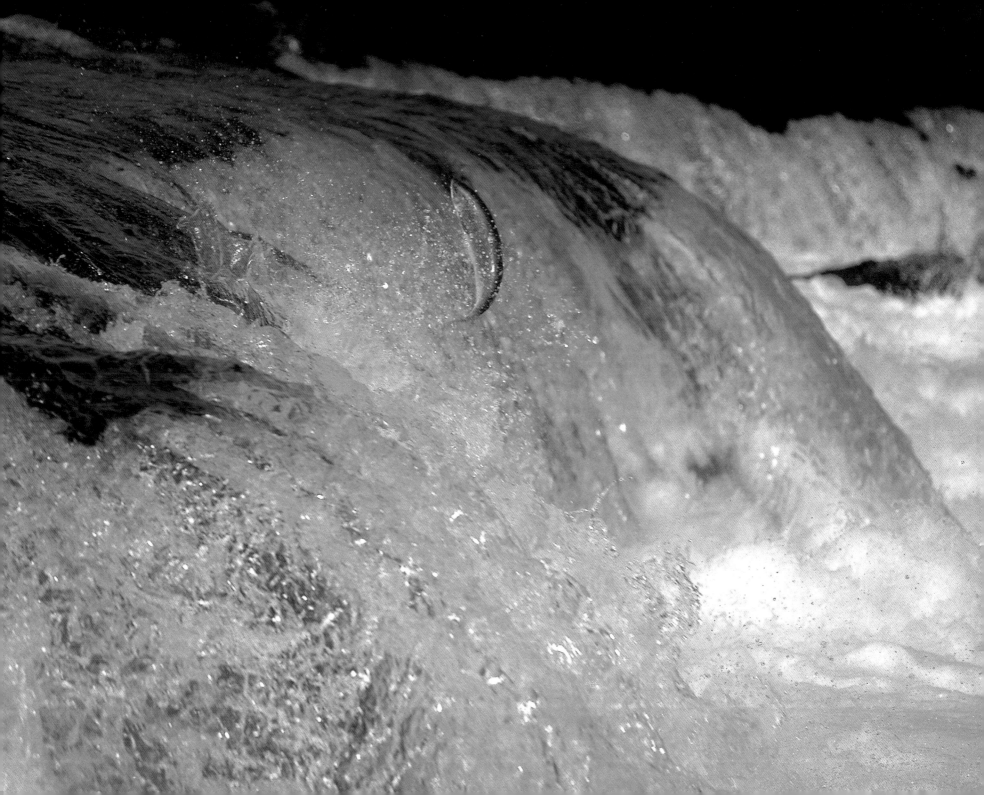

erupted. With ten times the force of the 1981 Mount St. Helens volcanic eruption in Washington State, Novarupta Volcano ejected some seven cubic miles of ash and pumice that buried the Ukak River Valley in up to seven hundred feet of volcanic materials. Enough dust was catapulted into the upper atmosphere to darken and cool the entire Northern Hemisphere nearly two degrees. Up to sixteen inches of ash fell on the nearby community of Kodiak, and residents found it necessary to burn lanterns in midday even though it was the height of the summer daylight period.

A National Geographic Society expedition visited the region in 1916 and 1917. Even four years after the eruption, the landscape appeared nearly devoid of life. After climbing Mount Katmai and viewing the ash-filled valley before him, expedition leader Robert Griggs described the scene: "The whole valley as far as the eye could reach was full of hundreds, no thousands—literally tens of thousands—of smokes curling up from its fissured floor. It was as though all the steam engines in the world, assembled together, had popped their safety valves at once and were letting off surplus steam in concert." The explorers used the steam coming from the holes to cook their dinners. The temperature six inches below the surface was 212 degrees.

The steam vents or fumaroles, as they are known, are now silenced; however, the descriptive name, "Valley of Ten Thousand Smokes," still applies to the region. Geologists speculate that the Novarupta Volcano eruption drained away magma from beneath Mount Katmai. The empty chamber collapsed in on itself, creating a caldera similar to that of Crater Lake in Oregon.

In 1918, shortly after the National Geographic expedition reported to the rest of the world, the entire area was set aside as Katmai National Monument. In 1980 the park was enlarged to four million acres to take in miles of fjord-studded coastline, several large salmon and trout-filled lakes, plus some fifteen active volcanoes. The park also provides habitat for North America's largest protected population of brown bears (grizzlies), which number about 750.

Katmai is one of many preserves in the region. Just to the north and 150 miles southwest of Anchorage lies the four-million-acre Lake Clark National Park and Preserve. Many consider this to be Alaska's most spectacular park, in part due to its diversity of landscape. Like Katmai, Lake Clark encompasses some active volcanoes within its boundaries, including the 10,000-foot-plus peaks of Iliamna Volcano and Redoubt Volcano. Both volcanoes have erupted a number of times since the Russians first recorded their presence, including a 1989 eruption of Redoubt. However, the centerpiece of the park is forty-mile-long, glacier-carved Lake Clark, nestled among peaks of the Chigmit Range. There are several small villages and a number of fishing lodges located along the lake. With land ranging from tundra to coastal forests and ocean bays, Lake Clark National Park and Preserve provides habitat for a variety of animals, from whales to Dall sheep.

Much of the remainder of the Alaska Peninsula is protected as wildlife refuges. Immediately south of Katmai lies the 1.2-million-acre Becharof National Wildlife Refuge, which includes Becharof Lake, second largest in Alaska. Salmon and brown bear highlight this refuge—both are abundant. Just below Becharof is the 4.3-million-acre Alaska Peninsula National Wildlife Refuge. The refuge takes in miles of wild coastline, as well as active volcanos like Mount Veniaminof which erupted in 1983. Other refuges in the region include Izembek, which protects Izembek Lagoon, a major waterfowl feeding area. Many of the Aleutian Islands are part of the extensive Alaska Maritime National Wildlife Refuge.

Sandwiched in the middle of the Alaska Peninsula Refuge, and approximately 150 miles south of Katmai, lies Aniakchak National Monument and Preserve. The park is small by Alaskan standards, only 580,000 acres. Named for the six-mile-wide collapsed volcano, Aniakchak Caldera, the monument is typically hidden in mist and clouds. Few visitors have actually set foot in the caldera. The volcano last erupted in 1931.

Western Alaska

The Bering Sea dominates Western Alaska, which includes salmon-rich Bristol Bay, as well as the Kuskokwim and Yukon deltas and the Seward Peninsula. This is the heartland for Alaskan native people, most of them Yup'ik Eskimo. Western Alaska has the greatest number of villages and remote communities in the state. To those used to evaluating a region by its scenic qualities, much of Western Alaska may seem uninviting, but it is

Hiker above Kalsin Bay, Kodiak Island

Autumn along Koyokuk River and Boreal Mountains

rich in food resources, including salmon, sea mammals, waterfowl, and caribou. In pre-Russian days, this was undeniably Alaska's most densely settled region.

Bristol Bay is world-renowned for its salmon. The area's numerous lakes and famous rivers like the Kvichak, Nushagak, Togiak, and Wood all provide spawning habitat for literally millions of sockeye salmon, making this one of Alaska's richest commercial fisheries.

Beyond Bristol Bay lie the wetlands of the Yukon-Kuskokwim Delta, which supports millions of waterfowl. More than fifty villages, most of them with fewer than 500 people, line the rivers which are the region's highways. Boats in summer, and snowmachines over ice in winter, link the far-flung communities. Subsistence hunting and fishing plays a significant role in these communities. Much of this region is part of the 19.6-million-acre Yukon Delta National Wildlife Refuge, where hunting by native people continues. This refuge, as large as the state of Maine, is the breeding ground for 140 species of birds, including half of the black brant and 90 percent of the emperor geese found in North America. Other wildlife includes caribou, grizzly bear, red fox, and beaver.

The Seward Peninsula was the site of one of the most unlikely gold discoveries in Alaska. Prospectors returning from the Klondike gold fields in the Yukon found small amounts of gold on Anvil Creek near present-day Nome. Newcomers were too late to stake claims on the creek, but were told to go pan for gold on the beach. Some did. Much to everyone's surprise, the beach sands were loaded with the mineral. By the summer of 1900, more than 20,000 people were working the "golden sands" of Nome—or the miners for the money. Some fifty saloons catered to their thirst.

Today, Nome is better known as the finish point for the 1,100-mile Iditarod, a dog sled race that commemorates a 1925 dog sled relay in which diphtheria serum was delivered from Knik by Anchorage to Nome. The serum made it in time to stave off an epidemic. Today the race is a major winter event for Alaskans that garners media attention throughout the world. Mushers typically complete the entire course in eleven or so days.

The Seward Peninsula is also the location of the 2.8-million-acre Bering Land Bridge National Preserve. During the last ice age, sea levels were reduced sufficiently to expose a land bridge more than a thousand miles wide between Asia and North America. Across this bridge, many species—including caribou, moose, and grizzly bear—may have entered the New World. Following in their footsteps were human hunters.

The preserve is designed to protect archaeological sites that remain as evidence of early human occupation. Humans have occupied the region for more than 10,000 years. The area also contains volcanic craters and lava flows, some less than 1,000 years old.

Interior Alaska

Interior Alaska lies sandwiched between two great mountain ranges—the Brooks Range on the north and the Alaska Range on the south. Drained by the Yukon River and its larger tributaries, this heavily forested region encompasses one third of Alaska, and is a land of climatic extremes. Temperatures may soar to one hundred degrees in summer, but dip to fifty, sixty, or even seventy below zero in winter. Most of the region is relatively dry, with a minimum of snowfall and rain. Fairbanks, for example, gets slightly more than ten inches of precipitation annually, two inches less than Tucson, Arizona.

Though extensive glacial ice sheets carved up the highlands that fringe the region, the Yukon River valley escaped glaciation, even during the height of the ice age. The interior was a vast, dry steppe where large herds of grazing and browsing animals roamed. Today their frozen remains, including such ice age mammals as large-horned bison and wooly mammoth, are still being recovered from the frozen ground.

Great rivers carve the Interior, including the Yukon, Tanana, and Koyukuk. These rivers were the highways of the native people, primarily Athabascan Indians, who lived here at the time of Russian contact. Because glaciers did not disturb placer gold deposits, these same interior rivers were also the site of many major gold discoveries. River terraces at Fairbanks, Franklin, Circle, Steel Creek, Livengood, and many other interior locations yielded highly concentrated and easily recoverable gold deposits.

Most of these early gold-mining communities disappeared or shrank to near "ghost-town" status; a few, most notably Fairbanks, grew to become regional trade centers. Fairbanks got its start when riverboat Captain E.T. Barnette set up a trading post at the mouth of the Chena River in 1901. When gold was discovered by Felix Pedro, the trading

Pioneer Home, Baranof Island, Sitka

post was expanded, and Fairbanks soon attained "town" status. By 1910, more than 3,500 people called Fairbanks home.

Fairbanks is now Alaska's second-largest city—some 75,000 people live in the city and surrounding borough. Fairbanks is the service center for many of the outlying communities throughout the northern portion of Alaska. When residents in Point Barrow or in Fort Yukon need to do some shopping, it is Fairbanks that they fly to. Nearby military bases, along with the University of Alaska, also maintain Fairbanks's economic base.

One of the attractions of the interior is 20,320-foot Mount McKinley. Denali, as it is also known, is the highest mountain in North America and centerpiece for the six-million-acre-plus Denali National Park and Preserve. The park was originally designated in 1917 as Mount McKinley National Park, but only half of its namesake mountain was included in the park. In 1980, the park was expanded and its name changed to Denali. Denali, the Athabascan word for the mountain, means the "high one."

Most of the park is trailless wilderness; however, a dirt road, which provides spectacular views of McKinley on clear days, travels ninety miles through the park to Wonder Lake. Denali is indisputably one of the best places to see wildlife in Alaska. Visitors traveling the park road are likely to see grizzly, wolf, moose, caribou, and Dall sheep.

McKinley was named in 1896 for Presidential nominee William McKinley. The first attempt to climb the peak occurred in 1903 when Judge Wickersham was able to partially scale the glacier-clad mountain. But it was not until 1910 that the "Sourdough" party from Fairbanks reached the lower north peak. In 1913, McKinley's slightly higher southern peak was climbed by Hudson Struck, Harry Karstens, and Walter Harper, giving them claim to the title as McKinley's first official summiteers.

In the old days, climbing McKinley meant a long hike or a dogsled to the mountain base, and an even longer slog to the summit. Today a thousand climbers or more attempt to gain the summit—most flying to a starting point part way up the mountain. Even with this advantage, the Arctic-like conditions turn back many a climbing party.

Other federal preserves in the Interior include the 2.5-million-acre Yukon-Charley Rivers National Preserve. The preserve takes in a 128-mile stretch of the Yukon River from its entrance into Alaska along the Yukon border to the village of Circle, as well as the drainages of a number of tributary rivers like the Charley, considered one of the finest float trips in Alaska. The Yukon-Charley Preserve has one of the highest nesting densities for the endangered peregrine falcon found anyplace in the world.

Just below the Yukon-Charley Rivers National Preserve, the Yukon enters the Yukon Flats National Wildlife Refuge, which has an estimated 30,000 lakes, ponds, and sloughs within its eight-million-acre boundaries. The refuge was set aside to protect nesting habitat for waterfowl. The Yukon Flats Refuge is only one of a number of wildlife refuges in the region. Others include the Tetlin, Nowitna, Innoko, Kanuti, and Koyukuk.

Arctic

L ying north of the Arctic Circle is Arctic Alaska. The region encompasses an area that extends from the Brooks Range to the Arctic Ocean, from the Yukon border to the Bering Sea. The Arctic portion of Alaska is one of the least-inhabited areas of the state. A few communities like Barrow, Kotzebue, Noatak, and Anaktuvuk Pass lie in and about the region, but overall, this is a stark, cold land where the human presence has always meant a touch and go situation.

Today the Arctic is a land of contrasts. On one hand it has some of the most remote wildlands left in the United States, but it is also the site of Alaska's largest industrial development, including the Prudhoe Bay oil fields. Nearly all of the coastal plain is open to oil exploration and development. Indeed, the Prudhoe Bay discovery is only one of many oil and gas fields that have been developed in Alaska's Arctic. Only a hundred mile stretch of coast within the Arctic Wildlife Refuge is currently closed to oil development. Environmentalists want to keep this last stretch of Arctic coast wild and undeveloped, while oil companies, some native corporations, and many of Alaska's state officials (motivated by the generous 85 percent royalty on all mineral development on federal lands conferred by the federal government at statehood), favor greater development. The issue is not yet resolved.

Beyond the transient population of 3,000 to 8,000 oil field workers at Deadhorse near

Kugrak River Valley, Gates of the Arctic National Park

Arrigetch Peaks, Brooks Range

Prudhoe Bay, the community of Barrow with 3,000 people, largely Eskimo, is also the most northern point in Alaska. The sun sets on November 18 and doesn't rise again until January 24. But this is balanced by months of sun in summer. Barrow was a major whaling station in the late 1800s. Today, despite its far northern location, Barrow residents enjoy cable TV and public radio, while many homes are heated by gas from nearby oil fields.

The only other major community is Kotzebue. Served by daily jet service from Anchorage, this community of 3,800 people can hardly be considered isolated. It is a trade center for ten nearby villages, and is the largest Eskimo community in Alaska. It even has a community college and technical center.

As interesting as these communities may be, it is the natural landscape that people generally think of when you say Arctic. Centerpiece is the 700-mile-long Brooks Range. These mountains were extensively glaciated during the last ice age, but today have only a few relict glaciers remain. Despite their northern location, the range is today too cold and dry for extensive glacial formation.

Much of the range is protected in one manner or another as part of several national parks, wildlife refuges, or preserves. Starting in the east is the 19-million-acre Arctic National Wildlife Refuge, which includes the highest point in the Brooks Range, 9,020-foot Mount Chamberlain. The refuge was set aside to protect the migration route and calving grounds of the 160,000-member Porcupine caribou herd. But the refuge is also home to Dall sheep, musk oxen, moose, grizzly, and even polar bears. Over 140 species of birds have been recorded here.

West of the Arctic National Wildlife Refuge and the Trans Alaska Pipeline lies the eight-million-acre Gates of the Arctic National Park and Preserve. The park lies in the central Brooks Range, and includes the ragged granite pinnacles known as the Arrigetch Peaks. Six wild and scenic rivers lie within its boundaries. The park is a grand landscape, and home to grizzly bear, Dall sheep, moose, caribou, and wolf.

Immediately adjacent to the Gates lies the 6.6-million-acre Noatak Preserve. The 395-mile Noatak River, whose headwaters lie in the Gates of the Arctic National Park, is one of the least-impacted major river drainages in the United States. Other than an Eskimo village near its mouth, the entire drainage is uninhabited. The preserve has been designated a U.N. World Biosphere Reserve. Each year a few intrepid river recreationists fly to the headwaters of the river and float the river's length.

Just south of the Noatak drainage lies the Kobuk River. Not as remote as the Noatak, the Kobuk has a number of small Eskimo villages along its length. Located along the Kobuk's bank is the 1.7-million-acre Kobuk National Park. The park contains Onion Portage, one of the most significant archaeological sites in Alaska. Artifacts found here date back 12,500 years. But it is the Kobuk Sand Dunes with 100-foot dunes that attract attention. Looking like a mini-Sahara, the dunes cover twenty-five square miles south of the river.

North of Kotzebue is Cape Krusenstern National Monument. The monument protects the archaeological sites found on 114 beach ridges, reflecting changing ocean levels during the past 10,000 years. The area has records of human use for the last 4,000 years.

Alaska is indeed a landscape that one should visit. But be forewarned, as Henry Gannett suggested; once you see Alaska, few other parts of the globe will seem as rich in wildlife and spectacular and wild beauty.

Wetlands along Lowe River, Chugach Mountains